MASSIMO LISTRI - DANIEL REY

MARRAKECH

LIVING ON THE EDGE OF THE DESERT

images
Publishing

First published in Italy in 2005 by
IdeArte srl - Via Regia 53, 55049 Viareggio, Italy
info@ideabooks.com - www.ideabooks.com

English edition published jointly in Australia in 2005 by IdeArte srl
and The Images Publishing Group

The Images Publishing Group ABN 89 059 734 431
6 Bastow Place, Mulgrave, Vic, 3170, Australia
Tel: +61 3 9561 5544 Fax: +61 3 9561 4860
books@images.com.au www.imagespublishing.com

ISBN: 1 86470 152 8

10 9 8 7 6 5 4 3 2 1

Designed by Marco de Sensi
English translation by William Larson
Printed by Stamparte, Italy

IMAGES has included on its website a page for special notices in relation to this
and its other publications. Please visit www.imagespublishing.com.

Printed in Italy

Front cover: Ksar Char Bagh   Back cover: Ríad Frans Ankoné

CONTENTS

LIVING ON THE EDGE OF THE DESERT

In its first twenty five years of existence, *AD Architectural Digest* has encountered and documented thousands of homes, rooms, stories, lifestyles and, even more importantly, made an equal number of friends. The fact is that many people have made the magazine's philosophy their own, including its ability not only to record variations in taste, but also to promote them and design new scenarios for living, sometimes recovering those of the grand tradition. Some of these friends have gone further yet, contributing to the defining of its style by bringing their own aesthetic sensibility and passions to it. Massimo Listri, the now famous Florence photographer, is assuredly among them, as is Daniel Rey, one of the great travellers of our time and unequalled virtuoso in the art of "drawing out" the soul of every place visited. And so it is hardly by chance that they are the authors of this magnificent volume, one responsible for the images, the other for the text.

But let us turn first to Listri, among other things because our lasting friendship and professional ties date all the way back to the maiden appearance of *AD* in 1981. For Listri, the pages of the magazine have represented a fertile laboratory for ideas and experimentation, enabling him to discover and then refine his highly personal expressive language to the point of writing a new chapter in the photography of architecture. A man of temperament, talent and imagination, Listri is also a sophisticated interpreter of the anthropological philosophy that informs any furnishing no matter what its orientation may be. With his elegant way of framing a subject, classic in its search for a visual absolute, Listri always succeeds in creating a game of mutual seduction between feeling and reality or, better yet, between image and architecture - both interior and exterior - grasping and then making perceptible the secret fascination of this affinity. What is involved is not just an aesthetic gift for its own sake (which would already be a great deal). Being curious by nature and constantly on the lookout for creative stimuli, Listri has made this approach the informing principle of his work, a formidable instrument for sounding the subtext and hypertext of any construction. And – now we come to the merit of this volume – it was in the process of meditating on ways of living in different parts of the world that he was among the first to discover the infinite charms of the so-called "ethnic style," training his lens on a world that is apparently almost overly familiar, but whose intimate essence is still largely unknown to the West. In his case, this interest gravitates mainly around Morocco with its distinctive atmosphere composed of the glowing colours that dazzled Delacroix and Manet, the intense and inebriating perfumes, the proud people, burning sands, cobalt skies, rows of ochre walls, the discrete white houses huddled in the dense network of city streets or scattered in the quiet of the countryside. The scenario is exotic and magical, so extraordinary that one might call it indescribable and unreproducible were it not for the fact that Listri manages to convey the wonder of it all through a lens that at once documents reality and moves the viewer. Page after page, the photographs that form this book transport the reader into a dream world of enchantment and yearning reflected in the silvery waters that shimmer in the rectangular basins of the patios and the *hammam* of apartments out of the *Arabian Nights' Entertainments* or in the luxuriant residences of the imperial cities, vivid reminders of a mighty culture and millennial traditions, or yet again in the mysterious and fascinating settings that throb in the "exclusive" and eccentric life narrated by Paul Bowles in *Tea in the Desert*. The journey evoked by the *imagerie* of Listri and accompanied by the masterly commentary of Daniel Rey is, then, absolutely exceptional. For two reasons: because of the evocative power of every image, and because each of them provides an occasion for better understanding the hidden facets of a formidable civilisation that is still largely problematic for us, suggesting a "noble" way of communicating and dealing with it.

Ettore Mocchetti

Editor of *AD Architectural Digest Italia*

Marrakech

In the course of his travels in Morocco, Pierre Loti often had occasion to praise the charm of the twilight hours. "This place, more than any other, has a special gift for concealing poverty, almost as if to heighten the natural beauty that cradles the country." The dusk – that daily adorns the "red city" with the richness of its chromatic range and paints it in the unique, deep and limpid colours of the desert, warm and intense – made it the chosen land of the poet. "Desert" is the magic word of Marrakech, the element that from time immemorial has never ceased to shape its history, fix its identity and mark its existence, especially when dusk – accompanied by its faithful servant, the warm breath of the Chergui – falls over the ramparts and penetrates into the *medina*.

Suddenly Marrakech falls silent, holds its breath, divests itself of its worldly ways and reverts to being what it really is, a "Daughter of the Desert," at once Berber and nomad, prone to the laws of nature and ready to exult in celebration of the end of the day, to bid goodnight to the sun sinking into the haze of the plain of Haouz with the same vital explosion witnessed by the blue Tuareg people as the ball of fire disappears into the dunes of the Sahara. Magic, enchanted moments. With the coming of twilight Marrakech gives itself up to all manner of seduction, the senses discover the thrill of happiness. On the horizon it seems that all the purple in the world, in its infinite shades, has chosen the Atlas chain as its domicile, and that the snowy crowns atop the peaks have been exchanged for so many gilded turbans. In the sky above the gardens of the El Bahdi palace, the swallows and storks stop bickering to trace improbable arabesques in the air.

Finally – but actually foremost – there is Koutubia, the mosque and beacon of the city, the tawny ochre queen, dominated by the Jaimur, the scintillating gold globes, where in former times the Islam faithful placed their offerings to Allah. This is the mosque where, from the height of its minaret, the end of the crepuscular spectacle is decreed. An age-old scenography, tried and true. Once the sun has disappeared from view, the silence becomes complete with a moment of absorbed suspension to better savour the solace promised by the prayer.

ALLAH AKBAR, ALLAH AKBAR, "Allah is great," cries the muezzin from atop the mosque. The prolonged call goes out at the speed of lightning all over the medina. ALLAH AKBAR rings out from the two hundred mosques of the city. A shiver runs up and down one's spine: the hour has come for the fourth prayer of the day, the time when Marrakech dons its finest garb to pay honour in Djemaa El Fna square, a stage that in the past was reserved for public hangings. Today it instead provides the setting for the spontaneous, unreal, ecstatic spectacle staged every evening – a magnificent popular performance rooted in the Middle Ages. It is the triumph of the irrational, of the timeless. The prayer concluded, Marrakech is transformed into the capital of the anachronistic. The population pours into the square, ready to commune with the masters of ceremonies of Djemaa El Fna. The improvised actors, disciples of the ephemeral, narrators, musicians of the Gnaua tribe, magicians, fortune tellers, combination apothecaries and healers with pockets full of magic potions, toothdrawers, snake charmers and monkey trainers, are all guided by the same will – a desire to humiliate poverty. Shouts and laughter, noise and smoke reign in the middle of the night as the square is engulfed by a riot of smells, images and sounds; those present are nearly hypnotised, verging on a state of trance. UNESCO was right to recognise Djemaa El Fna as a "masterpiece of the oral and spiritual heritage of mankind."

How remote is the time of the founding of the city almost a millennium ago. Then it was a dreadful, insidious place where no one lingered, so great was the fear instilled by the Berber dynasty of the Almoravidi, come from the Sahara to practise magic and sorcery.

People to avoid: the nomadic Masmudah tribe used the expression *marrakouch* to advise others to hasten away, a word that over time has been corrupted into *Marrakech*. Having found a name, the "Daughter of the Desert" still had to be given a soul and imparted the same religious rigour celebrated in Fès and Meknés. This was accomplished with the advent of the Almohadi dynasty, which gave free rein to the *ulema* reformers, authentic orthodox champions of Islam, animated by an extraordinary yearning for purification. At the time of their arrival, Marrakech shone with palaces and ramparts in the Hispano-Moorish style, testimony to an Almoravidi empire that extended from Spain to Algiers.

A sinful architecture, proclaimed the followers of Allah, who set about razing numerous buildings erected by the Almoravidi to make room for the architectural genius of the Almohadi dynasty, which proceeded to build the loveliest buildings of present-day Marrakech, one of them being the mosque of Koutubia, a gem of Hispano-Moorish art that served as a model for the construction of the Giralda, Seville's cathedral. The medina is the heart and also the soul of the city, an endless labyrinth of dark alleys, covered passages and tiny streets so narrow that not even the sunlight can penetrate; this is austerity itself in all its splendour. Here time and history leave no trace: here men whisper in undertones among themselves, move out of the way at the cry of *balek, balek* ("look out, look out"), race down the alleys on muleback, become animated at the call to prayer, pop out to buy a bunch of fresh mint, live shut away, surrounded by mystery and medieval rhythms in a universe "that must not be exposed to the offences of the street." It is on this subtle thought that all the architectural concepts of the medina hinge, including the houses of earth and brick, unadorned, with simple façades, perforated by rare windows and anonymous main doors of solid wood studded with nails. No ostentation, no hint of luxury, and yet this is where the Marrakech of the sultans flourished

and the *caid* caused the world to marvel with their fêtes straight out of the *Arabian Nights*. Has this Marrakech disappeared, along with the harems and the beautiful odalisques? Try opening the doors of these anonymous façades and – lo and behold! – the customs and legends of a hidden past come alive again. All it takes is the time to walk through the traditional *setwan* of Arab dwellings – meaning the dark zigzag corridor that prevents indiscreet eyes from violating the intimacy of the place – and you will find yourself in the paradise promised in the Koran. The paradise of Islam is a garden: "a sheltered corner of peace and freshness, where a thousand essences are found, an Eden disturbed only by the singing of the birds and the sound of water splashing in the fountains." The charming patio garden is a gem of Hispano-Moorish culture, also known as Wast ed dar, the centre of domestic life, where the special wellbeing that pervades the homes of the medina of Marrakech is found. This centuries-old type of housing – called *dar* if the owner's status is modest and *riad* if he is well off – obeys the Islamic precept that "beauty is the fruit of order." While little imagination and boldness were called for, much charm and harmony were required by the *maalem* of former times, meaning the master craftsmen whose task was to interpret the decorative needs of home owners, including covering pillars with *zellige* and ceilings with wood painted in the *zouaqué* style, in addition to decorating the walls with bas-reliefs of chiselled plaster. Once the work was finished, Marrakech's preoccupation with dedicating itself with pleasure to sorcery and occult sciences remained to be fulfilled. Upon entering a newly built home for the first time, for example, it was necessary to take infinite precautions, such as having a young virgin cross the threshold, followed by the owners, who took care to step inside with their right foot while invoking God to remove evil. The doors were opened to let the genies out and salt was poured in the corners of the house. The poor would sacrifice a chicken and the wealthy a ram. Then it was time to go through all the rooms burning incense and declaiming verses of the Koran in the expectation that the neighbours would come and offer dinner featuring *bciça*, a chicken cooked in incense over an aloe fire. The ancient rites are rarely observed today and unknown to the new pashas of the medina, the Western travellers who, won over on their way through the desert by the beauty and gentle grace of the city dubbed the "Baghdad of the West," decided to set down their suitcases. These people are the safeguard of Marrakech, forming a colony of the enlightened who resist the ancient adage stating that the "Daughter of the Desert" of water born, by water must perish. Underlying the adage is the fact that the city arose thanks to the presence of the water table associated with the Atlas Mountains, in effect cradling the city, while the rains condemn it by irreparably eroding its architecture of clay, stones and straw. In the *dar* and *riad* the struggle goes on against the inexorable, in a successful battle against the forces of nature. Restoration and repairs are carried out, embellishments are added, colours faded by the desert dust are brought back to life, the neglected patio gardens are revived, jasmine and oranges are given the proper care so that once more their blossoms release their fragrance – and most of all, so that when night falls the people again thrill at the thought of the Oriental delights awaiting them. A feeble light illuminates the sky, the sound of Andalusian music and the shouts of the Gnaoua singers can be heard coming from the *riad* …

In Marrakech some unlikely modern pashas thrive, all as intent as their predecessors on celebrating the prestige of a city that has given its name to a realm.

THE ANCIENT MEDINA

RIAD ARGANA

The passion for Marrakech, including love at first sight on the part of first-time visitors, has been attributed to a singular cause: magic. For some, Marrakech's rare power of seduction lies in the palm-groves, prelude to the immensity of the Sahara Desert, while others say the spell is rooted in that secret and unsettling court of miracles, the medina. Among the first to fall under the city's spell, long before it gained its worldly reputation, was the Marquis Louis de la Bleutière, a traveller attuned to nuance. The marquis is a man who weighs his words. "It is true that Marrakech captivates on first impact, but those with time enough to give themselves up to leisure are able to experience the full magic." By this he means an exquisite blend of "decadence and splendour, dust and colour, music and perfume," the six elements that mark the quotidian at the riad of Louis de la Breutière. Situated in the vicinity of the Mouassine fountain, it stands witness to the wealth of the Alaouiti dynasty.

The informing principle of the restoration was to transform the dwelling without doing harm to its soul. "All I did was recover the warmth of the original architecture with its sensuality, plus add a fresh touch here and there, like a Pointillist painter." In this sanctuary of exotic classicism the winds of modernity are barely perceptible. What little there is has been blended with the past, integrating it with traditional elements of Moroccan decor. The most tangible sign of this successful approach is undoubtedly the *sahrij*, the basin and swimming pool fit into the *bahou*, a niche, where one can relax out of the sun, that is easily mistaken for part of the original. The miracle is the work of skilled local craftsmen with the ability to disguise new additions with the patina of time. Anyone entering the salon of Riad Argana for the first time will be met with a challenge posed by the marquis. "Try to guess which of the decorative architectural elements do not date from the last century." Scrutinising the walls, there can be no doubt that the stucco friezes, bearing engraved and sculpted verses from the Koran, express the desire of the pasha who originally lived in the riad. The *tagguebbast* or edges of chiselled plaster lack the brightness they must once have had. The *testir* or geometric ornamentation of *zellige* that protects the base of the walls shows signs of dampness and winter cold. Above the doors, the uprights of the *chamachât* – the shell-shaped windows used for ventilation – bear traces of the abrupt changes in temperature typical of Marrakech. All that remains is a small fireplace finished with *tadelakt*, a coating of lime mixed with natural pigments which, when rubbed with a black soap, takes on the appearance of marbleised leather. Unless one is a true connoisseur of local culture, Louis de la Bleutière will emerge the winner. It is the fireplace that is of recent manufacture, being unknown to traditional Marrakech architecture. But the genius of the craftsmen who created it also reflects their natural inclination to avoid doing wrong to the spirit of the place – just as the marquis wanted.

The *zellige* on walls, floors and pillars form strictly geometrical patterns, in accordance with the dictate of
the Koran forbidding human or animal figures, thus preserving the principles of Islam.

Riad Obry

Abutting the palace of the pasha Glaoui in the medina of Marrakech is a *derb* or quarter called Mouassine, where life is steeped in age-old silence and mystery. In that maze of narrow streets and covered passages human figures stealthily come and go like ghosts. But this hidden side of the "Daughter of the Desert" also contains some of the loveliest *riad* in the city, almost all of them currently owned by famous designers and stylists. Nowadays, in fact, some refer to Mouassine as the "Fashion District." At nightfall torches light up the streets and gallant hosts dressed to the nines prepare to receive famous guests. Once underway, the parties last until the wee hours of the night and beyond. One word that has been used to describe them is "delirious."

There can be no doubt that the behaviour of this throng of celebrities represents a challenge to local tradition. Marrakech has learned to ignore the situation. It is, after all, thanks to these people that the "Red City" has been cleared of its ruins. This rebirth has its impudent aspects, such as when architecture on the edge of the Sahara is interpreted according to the latest trends in Western design. However, nothing but praise is due when the remodelling is inspired by discretion and respect for the past. Anyone who intends to live in Marrakech is forced to come to terms with the scourge of dampness. From time immemorial the patio fountain has been the only place used to get rid of wastewater, a system with magic overtones deemed useful for banishing misfortune. All this is not without its dramatic aspects for a medina built without foundations and which for extended periods lacked a proper sewer system. Today the subsoil underlying the heart of old Marrakech resembles a water-soaked sponge. The palaces languish, the riad give way and the medina waits to be saved, imploring pity. Oddly, negligence played a role in the restoration of the riad of Ralf Obry, who together with friend and architect Bjørn Conerdings made dampness the very essence of the rebirth of the dwelling. Right from the time work got underway, neither one had any doubt that it was necessary to conserve the traces of the riad's pain. The walls were swollen with water and the marble of the *tedlakt* finish was in a similar condition, while the pillars covered with *zellige* resembled abandoned games of patience. Most of all, the saltpetre gave off a powerful glow that could only be termed ominous. The architect faced a titanic job fit for a mole in trying to rectify the situation, which involved tunnelling underground to drain the subsoil. Thankfully, above ground the sun did its part. Upon completion, the restoration won general applause, and specifically from UNESCO, the organisation responsible for keeping watch over the conservation of the medina. Despite his passion for modern art, when it came to furbishing the riad, Ralf Obry curbed his impulses. "The most beautiful object in my home," he says, "lies in the walls." It is pointless to look for the work of leading designers because the sole author of the ingenuous, surrealistic shapes encrusted on the *tedlakt* is the history of neglect in Marrakech.

In Riad Obry the numerous sources of light – contemporary chandeliers, Syrian candelabra, Aladdin-style lamps and Moroccan wall lamps – enhance a restoration inspired by reverence for the past.

Riad Enija

"Be patient, give proof of perseverance, show detachment in the regards of the cosmopolitan elite that has made Marrakech its favourite refuge, and Allah will help you. He will help fulfil your desire to purchase the paradise that goes by the name of Riad Enija ..." With these words, Aziz, the elderly guardian of the seventeenth-century dwelling originally owned by a pasha, took leave of Bjørn Conerdings, a Swedish architect, and his wife Ursula Haldimann, an interior decorator of Swiss origin. Both were taken with the same palace that a number of celebrities had their eye on, including Naomi Campbell. But the months turned into years and still the riad remained in a state of sublime abandon. Turtledoves perched high in the cypresses, while muffled sounds could be heard from the direction of the nearby square where slaves were once traded. The strong aromas of the bazaar filled the air of the patio. The old sun-swollen woodwork sighed and cascades of bougainvillea drooped languidly. The escape from time was complete. Perhaps it was no coincidence that the heavenly decision came hard on the heels of a comment made by Bjørn Conerdings: "Nobody can consider himself the owner of a like monument. The most he can be is its guardian angel." What Conerdings meant was someone able to assume responsibility for standing vigil over a living page in the history of Marrakech, an edifice attesting to the explosion of architectural magnificence three centuries ago with the rise to power of the Alawiti dynasty. Allah had made his decision: the wisdom and discretion of the foreign couple would be rewarded by a chance to purchase Riad Enija. The two of them were the only ones able to convincingly guarantee that the past history of the place would not be jeopardised by the vogue for contemporary Orientalism, which too often leads to the cancellation of refined ancient beauty owing to a failure to interpret Islamic culture, other than by focussing on its use of gold and light. Following the replacement of unserviceable ceilings and the consolidation of weakened beams, Bjørn Conerdings proceeded with a light touch to undo the unseemly effects of time and nothing else. "There is always something moving about the scars that age leaves on noble buildings." Riad Enija would continue its existence with the cracks in the walls, the holes evident in the window frames, the abraded chiselled stucco-work and scratched enamel of the *zellige*. As the architect is fond of saying, in order to respect authenticity, a "microsurgery restoration" was called for. His desire to respect the building's roots received full expression in the patio, an area of domestic life where the garden assumes, like nothing else in Marrakech, an almost sacred dimension, in accordance with the dictates of Islam. The result is an exquisite earthly image of paradise, where the silence is broken only by the gushing of fountains and singing of birds, unequalled sources of energy for the lady of the house, as well a resource for her decorative imagination. A bright splash of colour signed by Jacopo Foggini, a bold curve fashioned by the hands of Chantal Saccomanno, a pastel chandelier designed by Pier Lorenzo Salvoni – that is the extent of the departure from tradition in splendid Riad Enija. Islam has imposed its law even in the use of colour: white, symbolising purity; and green, symbolising devotion to the Koran.

In Morocco, as a matter of principle, the patios of *duria* and *dar* – simple dwellings
– are bare and without plants, while those of *riad* – elaborate dwellings – are authentic gems of botanical art, Koranic symbols of earthly paradise.

In Riad Enija daring furniture, avant-garde lamps, painted cedar ceilings and fine stuccoes merge the cultures of East and West.

Riad el Mezouar

Isbtinne, derb el Hammam: an enchanted name that conjures up visions of the seductive charms of odalisques and the inebriating fragrance of essences. Impatience to get there mounts as the taxi weaves its way through clusters of men and worn-out asses piled high with their loads, then slackens as the driver heads into the labyrinth of narrow streets in the popular quarter of El Hammam, a *derb* said to be the most variegated anywhere in Marrakech from the ethnic standpoint, and finally ebbs away as Isbtinne proves to be less enchanting than the name suggests.

The din is deafening; the scent of spices fills the air and clouds of dust rise from the flow of traffic. Trade is intense. Some people laugh, others shout abuse; this is the real Marrakech, at once thrilling and suffocating.

A certain amount of patience is called for! It is a relief when the main door opens to Riad El Mezouar, and a liberation to abruptly find oneself in the atmosphere of an Andalusian monastery, which is exactly what the riad's co-owners, interior architect Jérôme Vermelin and designer friend Michel Durand-Meyrier, have managed to create in their princely eighteenth-century dwelling, once the property of Mezouar, head of protocol at the royal court of Morocco. The rigour enforced at the time of the dignitary still holds sway today, expressed both then and now in terms of restraint. This is the soul of the building, and pains were taken with the present-day restoration to respect its history by refurbishing, rather than removing, reminders of the past. The one major change was the addition of a delightful narrow basin bordered with aromatic plants. The arrangement provides a refreshing, fragrant environment. The shimmering water reflects the immaculate whiteness of Riad El Mezouar. White, a rare colour in Marrakech, is a sublime feature of this architecture, lending a certain magnificence to its austere nature. It also provides an attractive setting for the co-owners to display their latest work, which includes furniture and decorative objects that draw on the Ottoman style and classicism without overlooking the Orient. This sometimes involves unlikely juxtapositions, such as the placing of paintings depicting Turkish sultans together with a Louis Quinze armchair and a curious round Moroccan table made of plywood. Outrageous touches, but a viewer is more than won over when, as the afternoon wanes, the white of the riad becomes deeper and tinted a rose ochre. It is then that El Mezouar carries one far away from Marrakech to Andalusia or a Dodecanese island. The splendour is complete. For a moment the ancient local legend comes to mind that tells of certain families that kept keys almost as talismans, since they opened no doors. What if the doors to El Mezouar remained closed forever to protect the treasures within? Forlorn hope! As the heavy cedar door opens again, the spell is broken, swept away by the hubbub of Isbtinne, derb El Hammam. Riad El Mezouar is soon a distant dream.

Ogees blending the forms used in the palaces of Indian maharajahs and Arab pashas are used to embellish the arcades of the patio of Riad El Mezuar.

Riad 72

How disconcerting in the beginning … and how much curiosity! Why 72? Ambra, Saphyr, Malia, Dama, Sara … With names that promise delight and intrigue, conjuring up bewitching odalisques, the riad of the medina have accustomed us to poetry.

"72" is instead the street number of a riad on a street named Arset Awzel. Why go looking for something fancy, owner Giovanna Cinel must have reasoned, when Moslem culture is so shrouded in secrecy and discretion? Nothing could be more anonymous than a plain "72" nailed on the door. Who would ever imagine that hidden behind the tall walls is one of the loveliest riad in all Marrakech. Certainly, it is situated in the so-called "Golden Triangle" of the medina, the early twentieth-century reign of one of the most emblematic figures in the history of the city, the omnipotent pasha Glaui.

The extra-high wall of Riad 72 suggests that someone close indeed to the ruler enjoyed this particular patio, a place of rare refinement – very close, in fact, to our idea of an earthly paradise.

Unlike other gardens where the vegetation grows in lush profusion, Giovanna Cinel's is the quintessence of harmonious rigour, conveying a deep sense of serenity that takes us far from Morocco to the quiet of certain spots in the Far East. Here at Riad 72 the foliage of banana plants and palm trees practically obscures the view of the sky. A trickle of water runs placidly in the channel dug in the ground.

Gnaua music plays softly to the twittering of birds in the surrounding silence. Silence, much silence, is at home here. But there is more to it. Riad 72 casts its spell on visiting travellers fond of things beautiful: writers, painters, designers, celebrities, all looking for that special atmosphere that sometimes can be found in just the right hotel with a milieu conducive to creativity. Such people appreciate the fact that here at the gateway to the desert the mythical Spanish inn has been revived. During the restoration process of the riad, in fact, a subtle vein of Iberian inspiration touched the spirit of Giovanna Cinel and was conveyed by her to the woodwork. With their deep brown patina, the bow windows, doors and windows recall the aristocratic dwellings of Andalusia. The dark patches highlight the Zen spirit of the riad and the pastel tones of the contemporary designer furniture by the leading names of Milan. Of course, Riad 72 is complete with a dream terrace, the commanding position of which assures that once dusk has fallen the view of Marrakech is beyond compare. From this vantage point the entire medina, stained with purple, is visible in all its ancient splendour. It goes without saying that the prospect has made this terrace a favourite setting for fashion photographers.

Coloured with natural pigments, the famous *tadlakt* of Marrakech, made using the lime of Safi, produce walls featuring a wide range of chromatic effects.

Riad Frans Ankoné

Frans Ankoné, stylist and creative director of Romeo Gigli, has always thought of India as an ideal source of inspiration and energy, and Rajahstan as the proper setting for indulging his fancy in the matter of interior decoration. But his work, which compels him to divide his time among Paris, Amsterdam and Milan, soon proved to be incompatible with plans to go live in the foothills of the Himalayas. His was a dream without a future. Where, then, to shed the tiredness of the West? Morocco had been an unexpectedly pleasurable emotional experience on his first visit back in the 1960s. Who was to say whether the medina was still intriguing – and a little disquieting? Who was to say whether Djema El Fna Square still retained its medieval character, so rich in colour as to suggest that India was not really very far away? Marrakech, as he was able to verify, had not changed, nor had his passion for that world diminished over time.

Everything considered, if a maharajah's palace was not a practical solution, a nineteenth-century *riad* would do as a refuge for exploring new decorative directions. An added attraction was that his friends Alessandra Lippini and Fabrizio Bizzarri had located their gallery, the Ministero del Gusto, just a few steps away. Whereas in nearly every riad it is the natural tints of Marrakech – the thousand shades of red and ochre – that condition the chromatic effects of restoration, in the case of Frans Ankoné his love for India imposed its law.

Blue dominates unchallenged, applied to the *tadelak* in its full range: royal blue, turquoise, Indian blue-green, violet – a daring choice that the homeowner has artfully managed to tone down by including the hands of Fatimah, the typical amulet of Arab culture, sculpted in plaster or encrusted with semi-precious stones, that have the property of keeping evil away. In this particular riad, they also attenuate the full force of all that blue.

A visitor's gaze ranges far and wide, touching on corners that recall sumptuous Indian palaces and luxurious Ottoman dwellings, then comes to rest on the remains of a Moroccan decor that contains the splendour of the Almohadi dynasty. Frans' *riad* contains few pieces of furniture, all designed by the Ministero del Gusto. "The symphony of blues needs to be enjoyed in the pure state, without interference," maintains the owner. It was around eight-thirty in the evening on the terrace that day, a time when the infinite purple shades of the sunset had worked their magic; the sky, now dark, took on a royal blue tinge, ultramarine blue, violet … Frans Ankoné brightened. That evening, in Marrakech, the red had faded away, leaving the final say to the colours of India.

The Indian inspiration of Riad Ankoné, evident in the colouring of the walls, also includes Moroccan features. The lamps and torches were crafted by artisans from the bazaars of Marrakech. The fireplace by designer Alessandra Lippini incorporates forms dating from the 1980s designed by American decorator Bill Willis.

HAREM BAB AYLANE

Bab Aylane, one of ten city gates to the medina of Marrakech, meaning one of ten breeches in the ramparts, introduces you straight into the most secret part of the city, the slums where tourists still dare not venture and where signs appear on street-corners, warning "Non-Moslems Forbidden." In the narrow streets everyday life goes on, as it always has, at a medieval pace. Here is where the most skilled craftsmen of Marrakech are to be found, legacy of a glorious era in the history of the quarter, which at one time was home to the most genial craftsmen employed at the Royal Palace. Moreover, Bab Aylane has a special significance in the history of the city due to the fact that at the end of a blind alley named Derb El Majjat are found the remains of the last harem of Marrakech. Here the memory lives on of the lovely odalisques stretched out on divans, ready to cater to the whims of the *caid* Bounimhha. The splendour and mystery of this little-known monument has never ceased to amaze, ever since it became the property of Dominique du Beldi, the French businessman who purchased the harem. This gem of Oriental art stands in the shade of ancient jacaranda, which played a decisive role in du Beldi's infatuation with the riad. The truth of the matter is that nothing had changed since the harem beauties departed; the *zellige*, painted cedar ceilings and the *tadelakt* on the walls teemed with memories. In the dim light of the huge rooms one had no trouble imagining audacious scenes worthy of Delacroix. At the entrance, an ancient pulley fastened to the ceiling testified to the ingenious device used by the master of the house to have himself fanned with ostrich plumes arranged overhead. Everything left behind was authentic, but what finally convinced Dominique du Beldi to buy the harem were the trees that turn lavender blue in fair weather. His interest in the history of the place intensified when in the course of repairs, a previously walled-up passage leading to the adjacent riad was discovered. Extended purchase negotiations ensued, as did research, in an attempt to discover the history of the second building and pinpoint its connection with the first one. It turned out that the secret passageway was used by chosen members of the harem to reach the *caid* Bounimhha in his private apartments located in a riad that even today attests to the opulence of the original owner. Whereas in all the medina's other palaces the rooms rarely exceed three metres in width, date-palm beams being unable to support a greater span of ceiling, in each riad of the harem the rooms measure six metres across. So rich was the *caid* that he could afford to have cedars growing in a forest near Fès felled for the timber needed for his project. The restoration Dominique du Beldi carried out was organised by a consummate craftsman, Sheriff Moulay Taïeb, descendant of one of the seven great saints of Marrakech, and executed with the lightest touch, amounting to little more than a thorough cleaning of a harem built one hundred and fifty years ago. Virtually no changes were made in the basic structure, there being no desire to dress up a monument whose best feature will always be its underlying history. The one major addition was a swimming pool. But it is probably only a matter of time before it, too, will be populated with the imagined beauties of the past taking their ease at the water's edge.

The high ceilings of this palace, rare in Marrakech, attest to the opulence of the pasha who had the last harem of the city. Being wealthy, he was in a position to go against custom and insist on having the cedar beams of Ifrane instead of palm.

For many years this doorway was walled up. At one time it allowed the master of the house to join his harem in the adjoining *riad*.

DAR MOUASSINE

Taroudant is not the desert, and yet the light, smells, colour of the earth, dust and wind leave no room for doubt: on the other side of the mountains surrounding the ancient city of the Saadidi dynasty lies the immensity of the Sahara. It is an invisible but perceptible presence, that passes on the first symptoms of that sweet malady known as *mal d'Africa*, a heady feeling of freedom that defeats reason and paves the way for the temptation to drop one's anchor in the most bewitching of continents.

A dozen or so years ago, Carole Blique and Erick Kolenc were infected by the disease. At that time, they were nearing the end of shooting a film, after which their Taroudant adventure would be over. After several weeks spent in contact with the desert, the thought of the return to Paris was almost too painful to bear. Both were in the grip of the African sickness. As the time to embark for France drew near, their stay in Marrakech became tinged with desperation. And the fateful question arose: "What if the flight left without us?" And so it did. The takeoff of the plane signalled the beginning of a treasure hunt for Carole and Erick. For days they would comb the medina in search of a *riad*, conscious of the fact that in the near future the ancient dwellings of Marrakech were destined to become an answer to the demands of tourism. For the first three days the African sickness merely kept them hostage in Morocco, but the certainty of having reached a decision from which there would be no turning back struck them the moment they ventured into the Mouassine quarter and a door of a dar was opened for them in the Snane *derb*. While not ostensibly luxurious, it was marked by the generous simplicity that makes one realise, "It's pointless to keep on looking, this is our dream house."

In Carole and Erick's case, it was an apparently modest building, concealed behind which were the traces of a curious past, as emerged during the remodelling. The painted woodwork, polychrome stucco-work, and geometric patterns of the *zellige* left no doubt as to the splendours of the past; it was evident that the judge who built the *dar* had an interest in the decorative arts and was comfortably off. This was a magistrate more feared than loved, whose professional career was definitely not above suspicion – so much so that he had an emergency stairway built to allow him to flee to the rooftops at the first hint of danger. The stairway came to light in the process of knocking down the bedroom wall. Conserved as a vestige of the past, nowadays it is the prominent feature in one of the rooms of the Dar Mouassine, which is the name Carole and Erick have chosen for their spotless and delightful hotel furnished with exquisite taste. Their desire to leave a native imprint on the decor, while at the same time not overlooking traces of the country's past as a French protectorate, has led them on a ceaseless quest for unusual objects, further whetting their appetite for visits to the second-hand dealers who throng Tangiers and Rabat, where at one time the colonial spirit reigned.

RIAD GIL RIBOVA

A remarkable rare gem of aestheticism, the *riad* of Gil Ribova shone in the middle of Dar el Bacha, the most aristocratic quarter in the medina of Marrakech, embellished by a set of splendid places that attest to the past hegemony of the pasha Glaoui. Here, in dwellings contained within the high walls, is where the notables close to the pasha once lived, while those surrounded by lower walls were used to quarter the guards. Such is the property owned by Gil Ribova, a prominent figure in the Paris fashion world and owner of Victoires boutiques. The riad, originally without pretence or decorative excess, had the peculiarity of being the partition of a *douiria*, tiny lodgings built around a patio, which traditionally is an indication of high social status. Only the truly wealthy could afford a douiria to accommodate the discrete presence of live-in servants.

After Gil Ribova entered the scene, repair work was executed – so successfully, in fact, that in the eyes of many observers the restored riad surpassed the old riad at its best. As one description put it, "It is the work of aesthetes inspired by the sublime." There is no doubt that those involved employed a felicitous blend of Hispanic-Moorish and Hellenic architectural features. The place is Marrakech, but the use of white is far more typical of the Cyclades on Aegean shores, which is especially evident in the patio of the douiria where the swimming pool is.

Instead of calls to prayer from the mosques, here the church bells of Santorini might peal and no one would be surprised. The bougainvillea blaze against whitewashed walls just as in Mykonos, while the pattern formed by the polychrome cement squares used for the flooring might be found in fishermen's homes in Tinos. "Allah Akbar, Allah Akbar," comes the call of the muezzin, bringing us back to the medina of the "Daughter of the Desert." Gil Ribova has used fine old draperies to enhance the interior, in keeping with his fondness for Oriental antiques and his professional background. One example is the linen curtains made by the embroiderers of eighteenth-century Fès, hung in the ogees of the first-storey loggia. The exquisite work, forming a refined decorative element, is concentrated in the main rooms tinted eggplant purple and blue. Here we find such fabrics spread on mantelpieces, hung on walls and covering poufs, all of which are the fruit of extensive searches in the bazaars of Cairo and markets of Kashmir. The surprising colour combinations they create, together with the Berber mosaics designed by Gil Ribova and the carpets of Chichaua and Taznekt, are a sight to behold. There is nothing pompous or excessive about the decor; rather, what we have is the harmonious result of an innate ability to combine different objects and colours – in a word, "to create riches out of the simple things in life." Gil Ribova's philosophy has led him to use recovered materials, even items considered defective, such as cracked *zellige*, imperfectly blown glass, denatured natural pigments and rusty iron.

One visit to the riad is enough to confirm the general opinion of the restoration: the aesthetic statement is bold, beautiful and unique.

A hymn to Greece, the decor of Riad Gil Ribeva includes ceramic floor tiles recalling the patterns in use on the island of Tinos. The whitewashed stone "divan" is reminiscent of the Cyclades and the immaculate walls of those found in homes on the Aegean.

RIAD LOTUS

Riad Lotus-Ambre or the art of travelling outside time. Getting there is no easy matter: one must enter the murky depths of a vaulted passage and continue until reaching the narrow street named Hay Nefriti, never touched by the full light of day. The next step is being engulfed by the frenzied sounds and lights marking the nearby square, Djema El Fna. A bewitching place, the medina, where one is deceived into thinking he has understood its true nature, only to round a corner into a blind alley where all certainties vanish at the sight of something totally unexpected. In an increasingly dim light, Hay Nefriti gradually narrows, finally to a width no greater than the height of a man. Have we lost our way? We retrace our steps, convinced that the Lotus cannot possibly be here in a timeless dimension. But the liberating coup de théâtre is close at hand. The door of the riad opens to reveal a long open-air corridor faced with *tadelakt* the colour of chocolate. To understate the matter, the restful atmosphere makes for a refreshing change. At last Lotus-Ambre receives us in a patio pervaded with the spirit of Japan, bordered with succulent plants and unusual bonsai oranges. The fresh oasis is surrounded by imposing crenellated walls pierced by ogees with echoes of India. The riad soon reveals its personality, which is at once anachronistic and sophisticated, more than able to please the demanding clientele co-owners Réda Benjelloun and Alberto Este cater to. The nonconformist essence of the place is the work of Antoine Van Doorne, a decorator much in demand today in Marrakech. It is doubtful whether anyone else could have pulled off the feat of creating not so much a hotel as a theatrical setting. Visconti would have appreciated Lotus-Ambre for the way it achieves elegance through sobriety and boldness without resorting to flashy ostentation. Lotus-Ambre's daring knows no bounds. The furnishings of the Marilyn Room, Goethe Room and Mao Room all include details that commemorate the life of these figures. In the case of the blond vamp this means filmy fabrics, while old Chinese accessories allude to the past national leader and pages yellowed with age recall the German poet. An intimate drawing-room provides the perfect setting for Pinto's style: the consoles and bookcases are undoubtedly by Bugatti, while the original baroque armchairs have been reupholstered with gold and green fabrics designed by Lelièvre to lend an impertinent Empire touch. The combinations of colours, styles and periods are always courageous, at times transgressive, but achieve splendid harmony at Riad Lotus-Ambre. The sand-coloured coffers trimmed in black also include gaudy combinations of dark brown, burnt sienna and deep purple heightened by black lacquers. Antoine Van Doorne has expressed his unquestionable talent for sober elegance by using the basic elements of the decorative arts of Morocco, *bejmat*, *zellige* and *tadlakt*. He turned to local workshops to exceed recognised chromatic limits, inventing new pigments in shades of brown, plum and mother-of-pearl, the very colours that define the style of Riad Lotus-Ambre – and create a slight sense of disorientation. It is the touch that visitors touring the riad call the "new ethnicity."

Douiria Yves Morgant

Mouassine, Bab Ksour, the Casbah: for many years these quarters of the medina were a sort of promised land for Westerners, where on the other side of massive doors stood sumptuous *riad* with a flavour of old Andalusia. Little by little the source began to run dry and the fancies of the so-called new pashas of Marrakech turned to other labyrinths, among them Douar Graoua, just a few steps away from the palace of the Bahia.

It is a *douar* apparently lacking charm, densely populated and always animated. In short, it is a quarter that ceaselessly expresses the most precious gift of the city at the desert's edge – its native talent for commerce. With its confusion, noise and dust, Douar Gradua will never be anything like austere, monastic Mouassine, and the idea of coming here to buy a *riad* seems odd, even if the old-fashioned Hispano-Moorish patios do abound in charm.

Yves Morgant well remembers the day when, while strolling aimlessly down a broiling street, he was smitten by the sight of a door ajar. Attracted as much by the beckoning shade as curiosity, he decided to step inside uninvited – a move that proved to be a stroke of luck. There a *douiria* greeted him, a tiny riad, waiting impatiently for someone to show up at its bedside and put an end to its agony. Silence, old woodwork swollen with dampness, brackish *zellige* … a touching simplicity pervaded the early twentieth-century dwelling.

After months of searching, Yves Morgant had found his oasis of peace. Encouraged by friend and interior decorator Maria Grazia Pattavina, he decided to renovate the douria on Indo-Oriental lines and to give the patio – an authentic gem ideal for contemplative moments – an atmosphere evocative of the colonial homes of Zanzibar and Mombasa. This was achieved by using transparent cotton hangings that swell in the breeze, wrapping themselves around the cedar columns. The end result was a source of pride, and further proof that nothing is impossible in Marrakech, above all for residents of Douar Graoua, populated by craftsmen with an innovative bent.

Their versatility brought a fresh decorative spirit to the douria of Yves Morgant, particularly in cabinetmaking. Up until that time, it would have been all but unthinkable for Moroccans to groove wood like the craftsmen of Kerala, invent lighting solutions, scrape cedar and give it a patina equal to that obtained by Mombasa cabinetmakers. But then Yves Morgant showed them his art books. Soon innumerable sketches appeared on workshop walls, wood shavings piled up and little by little India and its artistic culture began to spring up in the heart of Marrakech – all for the benefit of the douria of Yves Morgant.

The finely crafted nineteenth-century woodwork and light linen hangings around beams carved by Marrakech cabinet-makers lend this *duria* the atmosphere of a colonial villa in southern India.

DAR MARZOTTO

An affectionate smile, a friendly gesture: Madame Marta. For many years now the inhabitants, whether Arab or Berber, of the quarter near the mosque of Bab Doukkala have considered her one of their own. The notoriety and aura surrounding her count for little here, owing to Marta Marzotto's winning ways based on an unaffected approach that has made respect the key to her lifestyle in the city of red. This respect is not limited to the people of the quarter, whose daily existence is often bound up with poverty, but also includes the local culture, shaped centuries ago at the time of the Almohadi dynasty and its redoubtable builders. When she took possession of her *riad*, Marta Marzotto was unwavering about how to redecorate it – or rather, rebuild it, because once the property changed hands she virtually had it razed. For once, American architect Stuart Church was compelled to set aside his infatuation with India and concentrate on a restoration with Marta Marzotto in mind, that would have to be in keeping with Islamic art and the decorative tradition of Morocco. For Stuart Church, this was an occasion to renew a long-dormant passion for journeys that lead to the discovery of other cultures and the way they influence art. Marta Marzotto invited him to explore the places where the treasures produced by the genius of the Almohadi are to be found: Tetuan, Tangier, Fès with its splendid Nejjarine fountain, Salé with its exquisite lace from the merinide period that covers the *madrasa*, Rabat with the stuccoes and *zellige* of the magnificent Dar Es Salam palace, Marrakech with its Stinyia and exuberant *mouqarna* or painted wood ceilings. Having completed his survey, Stuart Church then had to find a way to amalgamate the accumulated treasures and give Marta Marzotto's *riad* a lived-in look, in addition to a preciousness and voluptuousness worthy of a pasha of yesteryear. The outcome was extraordinary. Church managed to elaborate a highly refined ornamentation that restores to their ancient splendour the Moslem plastic arts in architecture, calligraphic decoration, floral arabesque and geometric patterns. In accordance with Almohadi principles, the walls of the residence are covered with Islamic inscriptions – but not the floor, the reason being that the ancient dynasty abhorred the thought of anyone treading on the sacred scripture. The great rooms for receiving visitors – not without their ostentatious touches – feature *zellige* wall panels that tell of an infinite universe of stars and arabesques that, drawing on the vegetable world and owing to Church's imagination, are enhanced with motifs inspired by Granada's Alhambra. In a *riad* frequently cited as an example of a restoration respectful of tradition, the architect has in reality left a personal imprimatur recognisable to an expert eye. To be sure, the *zuak* – the painted wood ceilings – were executed, as in olden times, using brushes made from donkey hair, but the ersatz concepts leave no doubt as to their origin. The chromatics surprised even Marta Marzotto. The bright hues standing in sharp contrast – including yellows, reds and greens – are far removed from the recommendations of the Almohadi, but close to those Church admires in India, his adopted country.

Dar Darma

Historians and art scholars say there is no doubt about it: the quarter where the Ben Yussef *madrasa* or Koranic school – an architectural gem going back to the era of the Marinidi – is located, represents the birthplace of the medina of Marrakech. And it is here where the evocative dwellings of the "Daughter of the Desert" stand. Behind high walls, the *riad*, *dar* and *duria* protect what is most majestic among the products of the city's history. Anyone who crosses the threshold of these buildings for the first time is in for a pleasant surprise – even more so if the door involved happens to be the heavy one of cedar belonging to Dar Darma. The property is owned by two Italian decorators who hit on the idea that here was an ideal place for creating a subtle play of colours and shapes, materials and lights, space and time.

The reaction of a person entering the patio is one of wonder and admiration. One is greeted by a pool of light of such monastic rigour that it would not appear unusual to see a monk pass under the arcades. There are neither trees nor flowers; here the fantasy of an earthly paradise is banned. All that remains are the black and white squares of the chessboard pattern described by the pavement. This is restraint in all its splendour, a monkish atmosphere evidenced by six large terracotta jars standing by a refreshing basin. With a flight of fancy one might imagine that the monks used these containers to hold olive oil and water. In reality, the Minimalist decoration and Zen spirit characterise just the patio of Dar Darma. In the bedrooms and halls the two decorators have proved to possess a talent rare in Marrakech, that draws on their sophisticated sense of design and has recourse to a multitude of styles within a decor that annuls all references and sets aside all acquired notions. The neo-classic, baroque, Art Deco and orientalism are blended in a highly original synthesis that an aesthete might call a "triumph of daring." The wall covering, so different from the usual *tadelakt*, captures one's gaze. The two Italian artists have ventured – successfully – to use what might be called chiffon painting. This involves processing the layers of plaster with a thin fabric, the only way to obtain certain faded blues and linen greys, and give Dar Darma a rustic touch that is simultaneously avant-garde. The nostalgic atmosphere that pervades Dar Darma and nurtures its spirit is untouched by the chromatic innovations, the originality of the fiery red velvet and creased fabrics the colour of cactus, or the general aesthetic audacity. While the modernity sought after by the two decorators is palpable, it is invariably accompanied by centuries-old splendours and suffused with melancholy. The lovely coloured woodwork is redolent of the past, while the stuccoes seem to want to blow away the dust. The oak alcove, containing a bed and open in the direction of Mecca, seems to regret the passing of the time when the master used to come here to kneel in prayer. One looks on in admiration … and experiences infinite nostalgia. Opening the terrace door, one is seized by a feeling of freedom. And once again, here are the Atlas Mountains, the blue sky, and the hubbub of the city. Intentionally removed from the outer world, Dar Darma has for a time succeeded in making us forget Marrakech.

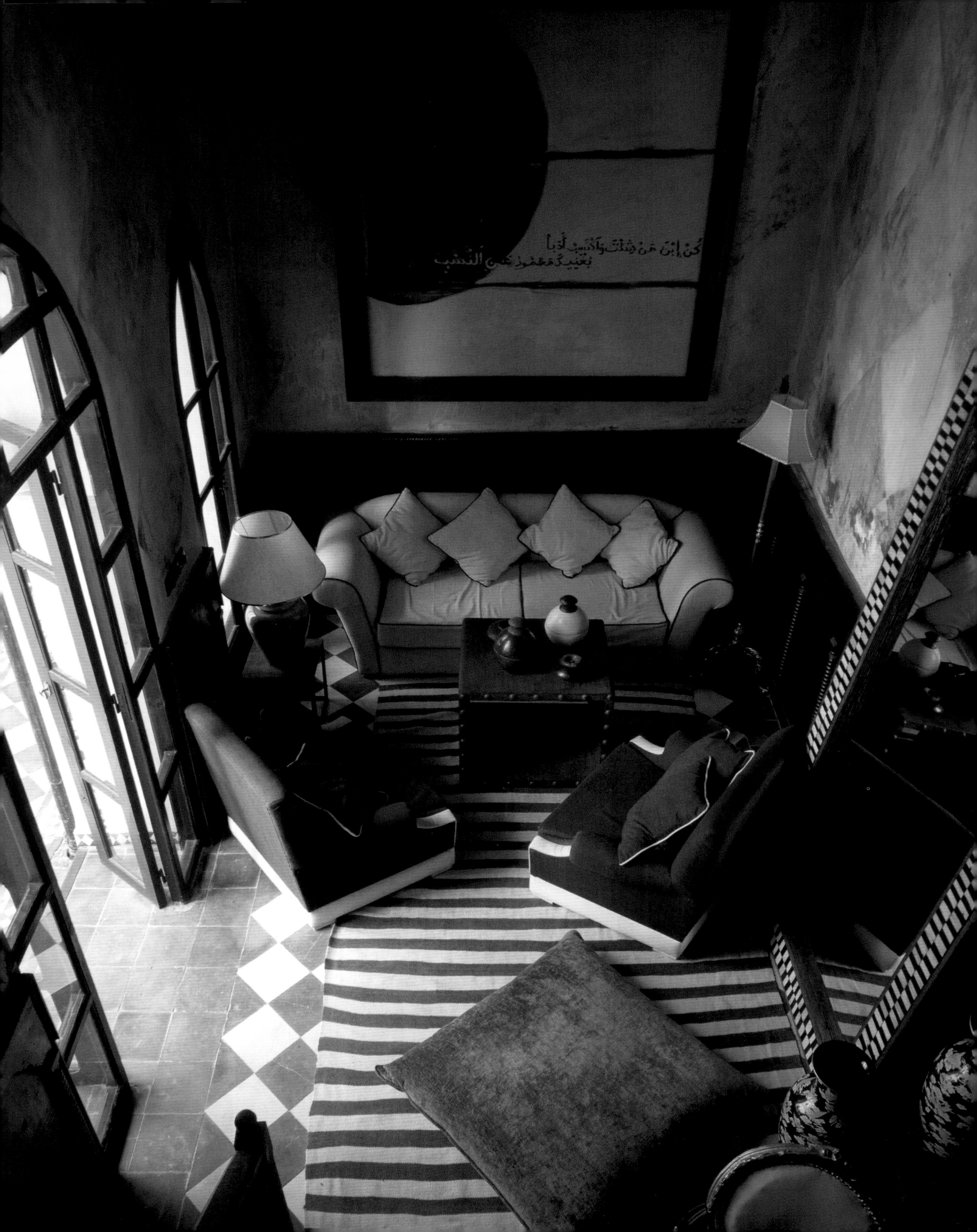
كن ابن من شئت واكتسب أدبا
يغنيك محموده عن النسب

THE MODERN MEDINA

Il Ministero del Gusto

Ten years ago in Bologna complaints were rife about how cold it was that winter. Fashion stylist Alessandra Lippini and interior decorator Fabrizio Bizzarri had nothing in common but their intolerance for the chill north wind and a mad craving to leave everything behind and recharge their creative energy elsewhere. Marrakech held the same fascination for them as it had for Paul Bowles, Yves Saint Laurent, Adolfo de Velasco and Bill Willis: an irresistible attraction, a disquieting return to the Middle Ages, a charm that captivates and seduces those active in the arts. In the aftermath of a felicitous encounter with the "Daughter of the Desert," the pair from Bologna considered joining forces. Why not? Together they founded an art gallery named "Ministero del Gusto," Italian for the Ministry of Taste. Today no one contests the fact that it is Marrakech's most innovative and famous.

It is a place removed from time, exempt from all the usual aesthetic principles dear to Western art galleries. No Zen, no clean lines. "Our exhibition space is a gesture of defiance," explains Fabrizio Bizzarri. And it truly was a challenge to open a gallery in the Derb Azur el Mouassine, at the end of a nondescript little street of the medina. The instant one sets foot in the establishment, the courage of the decision is immediately evident. The Ministero del Gusto is located in a tiny riad, where the rooms, bath, kitchenette and terrace form an unbroken space given over to art. Alessandra Lippini, who has done a fine job redecorating along multiethnic lines, managed the difficult feat of successfully accommodating the disparate decorative artwork of the Masai tribe and of the peoples of northeast Africa and Mexico. The result is convincing and alluring. Here and there the small fireplaces take the shape of primitive masks; a palm trunk acts as a shower bar; the foot of an elephant modelled in cement forms a bidet. The renovation is original to the point of constituting a leading feature of the gallery, on the same plane as the artwork on display. Honour is due the Ministero del Gusto as such. Respect is also due the unique, original creations it contains, that express pleasure in the artistic gesture of shaping matter and, even more frequently, the love for unusual combinations of materials, such as leather and iron, or wood and copper. One's gaze comes to rest on the figurative "savage" by Indonesian painter Bibka and the Pop Art silk-screens by Moroccan Hassan Hajiag, then moves on to works painted by French artist François Le Long, and the furniture created by the masters of the gallery, which blend ethnic spirit and contemporary lines. Such eclecticism fascinates connoisseurs and celebrities who have made the Ministero del Gusto a required stop in Marrakech. Normally a meeting place for the cosmopolitan elite, when Alessandra Lippini and Fabrizio Bizzarri decide to inaugurate a new show the gallery takes on a splendour reminiscent of a scene from the *Arabian Nights*. One looks on in admiration, amazed by what a chance meeting in wintry Bologna has led to on the edge of the desert.

The fondness of gallery owner Alessandra Lippini for ethnic art is reflected in the tiny *riad*, where the cultural products of Africa and Latin America mix, including tribal creations from Mali and architectural elements typical of Mexico.

Providing open space for shows, the gallery terrace is reminiscent of the huts of Niger, Mali and Togo, built using found materials (tin, iron, wood) incorporated in a simple construction of earth and straw.

Riad Pinco Pallino

Who says that fairytales are a figment of the imagination? The story that links Marrakech to Imelde and Stefano Cavalleri, holders of the Pinco Pallino trademark for children's clothes, has much in common with fairytales, and yet it is true. Several years ago, Stefano Cavalleri decided to depart for Morocco in search of new inspiration. At a certain point, he was walking in the medina looking for an art gallery that also features decorative objects, founded by Italians and called the Ministero del Gusto. Finally, in the dim light of a covered street, he ended up knocking at a door that looked right to him. What happened next was an extraordinary coincidence: although he did not realise it at first, there on the threshold appeared Alessandra Lippini in person, the founder of Ministero del Gusto. When Stefano asked her if he had come to the right address, he was amazed to hear a familiar voice answer. Looking closer, the face was that of a friend he had not seen for years. Naturally, the event called for a celebration, for which there could be no better place than Marrakech, where the joy of living is an art. It proved to be such a memorable evening. Between experiencing the mysteries of the Orient and the thrill of freedom, the thought occurred to him: "What if I were to stay on here in Marrakech?" A remark on the part of Alessandra Lippini did the rest: "Why don't you buy a *riad*?" Almost for the fun of it, the hunt began for a suitable place in the medina. But Stefano's fairytale was not over yet. Without breathing a word to him, his wife Imelde got it into her head that with Alessandra's help she would find the patio of their dreams on her own. Later that year when Christmas rolled around an unusual gift was waiting under the tree for Stefano: a sealed envelope containing the key to a riad in Marrakech. No kinder thought could have crowned their twenty-five years of life together.

"Goodbye, Alessandra, and be brave! We'll be back when the work is done. You know we've given you carte-blanche." And for the next year and a half the Cavalleri couple did not worry much about the riad, which was the time Alessandra Lippini and her partner Fabrizio Bizzarri required to translate the fresh winds blowing through traditional local architecture and decor into reality.

The baroque preferences of Stefano were rejected, while the Zen ideas of his wife were accepted. Both agreed on the colour scheme. Alessandra undertook the restoration guided by a single imperative: "stick to the basics." This included a constant awareness of the need to exploit the natural light, all too often at a premium in such dwellings. The designer's daring was admirable. Her convincing initiatives included the use of mother-of-pearl for the swimming pool bottom and trompe-l'oeil techniques elsewhere. She also had a way of mixing river stones and cement that was as unconstrained as it was successful. Her obvious sources of inspiration included the Bauhaus Movement, Mondrian (as evident in the reconstructed work adorning the kitchen) and Sonia Delauney (in connection with a cement 'carpet'). As the fairytale goes, upon their return Stefano and Imelde found only one way to show their gratitude: by standing in silent admiration.

In place of the traditional garden, the patio of this *riad* has a swimming pool wedged into the *bou*, a niche that characterises the more sumptuous palaces. Mother-of-pearl lining the bottom of the swimming pool produces a striking aesthetic effect.

An avant-garde *riad* with bold lines, Pinco Pallino displays a specific cultural choice in each of its rooms. Examples include the kitchen adorned with works recalling Mondrian and halls with echoes of the Bauhaus school.

OUTSIDE THE MEDINA

Ksar Char Bagh

In Arabic, "sublime" has a new synonym: Ksar Char-Bagh, the latest gem of the hotel industry of Marrakech – the quintessence of perfection, a masterpiece of refinement that appears at a bend in the path running through the palm-grove, conspicuous against the snowy peaks of the Atlas Mountains and reddish soil of the Chimlat hills. It is a mirage, a dream rising from the sand, a palace for exceptional guests conceived by Nicole and Patrick Grandsire LeVillair. Before undertaking this venture, the two of them had achieved success in Paris in the world of publishing and advertising. But mornings in Paris when they would throw open the shutters of their bedroom window, the horizon that greeted them was invariably smudged by the grey atmosphere. At that point a desire for something different insinuated itself: to live on light, to become inebriated with sunshine. Mexico? The Orient? No. Instead, fate arranged for the choice to fall on Morocco. As it happened, at the time a dear friend, Marcel Chiche, who lived in a lower flat in the same building, was busy completing Comptoir Paris-Marrakech, the temple of nightlife in Marrakech. Morocco could not have had a more persuasive spokesman. Pervaded with silence and drenched in light, the palm-grove cast its spell on Patrick, while Nicole began to weigh the pros and cons of the momentous idea of building a palace at the gateway to the desert. Lingering doubts were dispelled after a visit to the Paris Institut du Monde Arabe and its overflowing shelves of books and manuscripts on the treasures of Oriental architecture and Persian art, the divine gardens of Iran, the enormous wealth that had lit up the world of the fourteenth century and made possible the building of the mythical monument of Alhambra in Granada, icon of the period and sublime model that would inspire Nicole and Patrick. Ksar Char-Bagh, an old Persian name, was used to indicate a garden that formed the site of a palace and was the hub of watercourses and pathways. The choice of that as a name for the hotel was a natural, but the far more arduous task of integrating architecture, garden and water represented a challenge to tradition. Happily, the craftsmen of Marrakech rose to the occasion, creating a unique work, the likes of which had never before been seen in Morocco. Sixty stucco-workers were engaged for many months to fashion a lacy structure that withstands comparison with the Courtyard of the Lions and Courtyard of Myrtle at Alhambra. The multitude of workers was directed by successful Marrakech architect Akim Ben Jelloun, while naturally enough Patrick and Nicole were assiduously present, the former to supervise aesthetic matters and the latter in charge of bookkeeping. They were the real protagonists of Ksar Char-Bagh, being responsible for the creation of the Courtyard of the Gueiza, galleries of the *muqqarna* and unusual passages. Their determination to shun banality led to the idea of paving the floors with the brown stones of the Ourika River and plastering the façades using sand from the seashore with natural tints. "Art," they are fond of saying, "advances a step with Ksar Char-Bagh." A prestigious feature of their aesthetics is the water that surfaces after a long run from the mountains of the Atlas range, easily taking its place in and outside the palace in the gardens and halls. It murmurs in the fountains, babbles in the basins, managing to evoke the Zen spirit with a monastic sense of proportion. The guests speak softly, walking with measured steps; they take time to stop and experience the reawakening of the senses. There can be no doubt that Ksar Char-Bagh is indeed a new way of saying sublime.

AMANJENA

"To make others dream by drawing on the impossible" has always been the philosophy of the Amanresort hotel chain, because in this world of ours there is no such thing as a hidden corner or inaccessible spot. Wherever one goes, from the coral beaches of Polynesia to the impenetrable jungles of Indonesia, and from the islands of the China Sea to the wilds of Wyoming, an Amanresort hotel invariably pops up. The immensity of the desert was one of the few remaining places to be conquered. Thus, when the project for a new hotel, designed to be the pride of the company, was initiated, Ed Tuttle had no second thoughts. The genial American architect, nicknamed the "Livingstone of modern times" owing to his spirit of adventure and passion for travel, set out to cover practically every stretch of desert sand in the world, including in Jordan, Namibia, Chile and the Gobi – thousands of miles travelled in hopes of capturing a mirage and transforming it into a paradise able to meet the needs of Amanresort's guests. The long journey took him to a place in Morocco where the Dra and Dadés valleys merge with the immensity of the Sahara, and at last to Marrakech. Ed Tuttle proved no exception to the rule of love at first sight, realising that he had found what he was looking for in Palmeraie. There he discovered a centuries-old olive orchard reflected in the waters of a *sahrij* or a basin dating from the tenth century, the era of the Almoravidi. In the suggestive oasis the concept of *aman* – meaning "peace" in Sanskrit, life at its fullest – was palpable; the Amanresort Group is generally inclined to translate this into a Minimalist decor and Zen atmosphere. Ed Tuttle took only two years to complete his "hymn to creation," the Amanjena or the "peace of the gardens of paradise," a perfect synthesis of past and future, the grandiose and essential, antique and modern, handcrafting and avant-garde technology, but also a homage to a land that accepted a hotel in harmony with its traditional architectural lines, decor and customs. Even though it is a hotel, the Amanjena adheres to the rule of strict privacy, reminding us that in this context a dwelling is a place of discretion. Ed Tuttle carefully avoided any ostentatious decoration on the building's façade. But a traveller opening the heavy cedar door will be agog at the rare beauty of a sight marked by purity and restraint. Every nook and cranny contains reminders of the prestigious Arab civilisation of the past: the huge lobby, with overtones of a caravan inn of old, includes ogees suggesting the Mezquita, the mosque of Cordoba, while the colonnade running along the body of water that reflects the building is an echo of the Almohadi dynasty, responsible for the celebrated lake of the Menara of Marrakech. Here is a touch that immerses one in the magnificence that surrounded the life of the Almoravidi sovereigns, there something else that opens up the grandiose world of folly of the caliph Abd El Mumen. Ed Tuttle's work, characterised by magnificence unfailingly expressed with a light touch, embodies the broadness of the vision behind it. The architect has managed the unprecedented feat of infusing the Zen spirit into Arab/Andalusian culture. For those guests heading into the desert, Amanjena is the gateway to Eden, while for those heading back it is "the oasis at the end of the journey."

PALAIS AZIZ LAMGHARI

Unlike most Palmeraie complexes – triumphs of landscaping skills and the playing of fountains – the Palazzo Aziz Lamghari is set in untamed nature amidst lush natural vegetation. Here there are no aromatic hedges trimmed according to the rules or palm trunks entwined with bougainvillea or lawns. Lamghari receives you with the joie de vivre that distinguishes an untrammelled natural setting shaped by the blowing of the *chergui* and the plentiful underground water in the Marrakech area. A few steps along a dusty path bordered with a thick screen of bamboo, the tip of a nose becomes visible, which is actually the white summit of the cupola of the dwelling of architect Aziz Lamghari. This construction, the only one of its kind in Marrakech, is related to the monumental *marabout* or the tombs of the holy men who dedicate their life to the Koran. Anyone approaching is struck by this aspect. The temptation is to turn back, convinced that ordinary life would be impossible in a place with such strong religious overtones. The fact is that Lamghari, the most original Moroccan architect, has chosen this place to lead the retired life that suits him best, far removed from the outer world. If it comes as a surprise to discover that the exterior resembles a *marabout*, it is an even greater surprise to find that the interior is no different. The residence is a sort of monastery in the desert, a cathedral set in the Palmeraie. One is dazzled, amazed. To what lengths can the human imagination go? Aziz Lamghari is a world apart, punctuated by mammoth pillars that express the architect's passion for statuary art and colonnades, which he discovered in his student years in Paris at the Ecole des Beaux-Arts. At that time, he would spend day after day intent on drawing Hispano-Moorish pillars and Greek capitals of the type that would later become his signature as a professional architect with an interest in interior design. His own home is a composite of cultural traditions borrowed from different parts of the world. One's gaze encompasses the top of pillars of reinforced concrete, the Corinthian and Doric volutes, Gothic grandeur and Andalusian refinement. The perspective marvels are the result of careful study so that, far from being oppressive, they infuse an enormous sense of freedom. Seated in one of the comfortable armchairs typical of an English club, it is easy to become lost in reverie: the image of the Pantheon surfaces in one's thoughts, the Mezquita of Cordoba seems just around the corner: Greece and Spain. But when you go back again sometime you will find that everything has changed. Aziz Lamghari will have tired of Hellenic and Iberian reminiscences, and moved on to decorate his pillars with the splendours of ancient Egyptian culture and recollections of student days in Paris. "Cinema sets" … "stage scenery" … Until the moment when the house comes alive, one wonders how it is possible to live in such an outsized place, all the more so for a person who wants to live like a hermit. The answer is not long in coming. The strains of one of Verdi's operas reach us from somewhere beyond the pillars, the lights dim. This evening, yet once more, art, music and literature will be our faithful companions in a vigil dedicated to the pleasure of being alive.

Doric and Corinthian capitals, Greek and Egyptian pillars and Islamic ogees make this dining room a near replica of the Mezquita of Cordoba. This was the desire of Aziz Lamghari, known since his student days at the Beaux Arts Institute of Paris as "the columns architect."

VILLA MAHA

When Olivia Grigaux turned to friend and neighbour Aziz Lamghari, the architect who has made the monuments of antiquity his source of inspiration, the general conviction was that the fate of Villa Maha was sealed, meaning that once again traces of classical Greece would make their appearance in the heart of Palmeraie.

The early schemes the architect presented confirmed the fears. "The pillars man," as Lamghari is sometimes called, was about to give free rein to his passion. The fears proved unfounded because this time Olivia Grigaux' determination and profound knowledge of art history would manage to ground any rash flights of architectural fancy. Following her romantic bent, Olivia had her heart set on a dwelling in an Oriental vein, protected in back by the high walls of a façade reminiscent of the manors of Périgord and the medieval castles of Berry.

The result was a country house whose very name, Maha, pays homage to femininity.

Maha, synonymous with *biche* in classical Arabic, is a refined term that the pashas used in bygone days to refer to women. And in Olivia Grigaux femininity has found a devoted, loyal ambassadress, dedicated to cultivating whatever is surpassingly fine. In decorating her home, she introduced a typical feminine touch characterised by taste and sensitivity, the essential ingredients for a decor dictated by a desire for harmony. The colours and fabrics are in perfect equilibrium with barely a false note in the arrangement of the furniture and other objects that speak of her travels and stand witness to her predilection for the culture of India and the Far East. And so here we have the chests of drawers purchased in Rajasthan, the straw-bottomed chairs found on Hollywood Road, the reign of Hong Kong antique dealers, as well as a Chinese bed originally for smokers of opium, now used as a table, and embossed brass cases from Jaipur.

The good taste of the lady of the house has transformed ethnic decoration into a composition that she herself defines as "culture and history." These are interiors that fascinate anyone with a passion for art and a fondness for singular objects, such as the eyeglass cases of Indian silk placed on the windowsills.

Villa Maha is alien to excess, detests ostentation and prides itself on rigour, above all in the garden. Geraniums blaze under tall date palms; the cypresses soar perfectly conical as in Provence, where Olivia was born. The datura, too, have been shaped to suit the mistress of Villa Maha. Improvisation is not tolerated, except when it comes to the storks that appear every evening at dusk to make use of the property as a stage to revere the day as sunset draws nigh.

Riad Nicole

With its infinite space and virgin lands, Africa has always enthralled travellers. Many of them were pioneers, all of considerable stature, some of them famous, such as Pierre Loti, Karen Blixen and David Livingstone. Other anonymous figures stayed on to live with the Masai or Dogon tribes, or to dedicate themselves to the conservation of endangered species, such as the gorillas of Uganda.

In Morocco no one would think of belittling the gratitude rightfully due Meryanne Loum-Martin, who in 1989 introduced Marrakech to the concept, widespread in France, of the *maison d'hôtes*, or private home open to travellers. She was the first to realise that the magical, fascinating *riad* of the medina had the potential to become the Moroccan version of the successful French concept. Meryanne Loum-Martin's intuition proved to be stroke of genius, with the idea taking root and spreading to the point where today, years later, countless *riad* in Marrakech have been converted into delightful hotels.

Meryanne's father was from Senegal and her mother from the Antilles; despite her background as a diligent student at the Paris school of fine arts and a trained lawyer, since her youth she has had the soul of a globetrotter. But in view of the impossibility of heading off to the Antilles on weekends to bask in the intoxicating freedom of the Caribbean, and drawn to the lifestyle of Marrakech, where it is customary to pass the time in the shade of a veranda as in her native land, she decided to come to live in Morocco. Here she opened the first *maison d'hôtes* outside the medina – considered too suffocating – choosing the *palmeraie* as the place best suited to her desire for escape. Out of all this arose Dar Nicole, pervaded by an elegant simplicity embellished by the products of ethnic art that bespeak the owner's passions and attest to her deep knowledge of decor.

Success was immediate. Armani, Ferré, Missoni, Brad Pitt, Tom Cruise and Caroline of Monaco are among those who have fallen under the spell of a type of hotel otherwise unknown to Marrakech. But Meryanne's entrepreneurial spirit was hardly exhausted. With no desire to rest on her laurels, she proceeded to embark on a further innovative venture, creating a *maison d'hôtes* of an unusual kind in the palmeraie of Jnane Tamsna, namely a country guesthouse inspired by the Latin American *hacienda*, deliberately nature-oriented. Meryanne calls it "a new-generation riad." The Hispano-Moorish architecture she designed respects the traditions of Morocco, the major deviation being the large number of patios – "earthly paradises" – arranged one after the other, which form the soul of Jnane Tamsna, as well as its intellectual vocation. One way of summing up the place is to describe it as a private dwelling consecrated to culture, where guests are invited to share Meryanne Loum-Martin's passion for literature. Throughout the year the famous personalities who arrive at Jnane Tamsna are invited to take part in the stimulating literary salons conducted in English – further proof that the proprietor deserves her reputation as a pioneer.

The first *maison d'hôtes* opened in Marrakech, Riad Nicole speaks to us of the decorative predilections of the proprietor, Meryanne Loum-Martin, running from India to Africa, her native land. The sabra fabrics, cotton of Kerala, lamps and screens of Morocco, low table of Rajasthan and other old objects seem to invite guests on a journey without frontiers.

SERRA ADOLFO DE VELASCO

Yves Saint Laurent, Bill Willis and Adolfo de Velasco – the musketeers of Marrakech, three legendary personalities and the ambassadors of worldly Marrakech – have trailed cosmopolitan high society in their wake, which by now has left its imprint on the "Daughter of the Desert." While Bill Willis had eyes only for the *riad* of the medina, de Velasco and Saint Laurent preferred to establish themselves in the Guéliz quarter, a peaceful corner adjacent the Majorelle gardens, where houses are hidden in the luxuriant vegetation planted by the painter Majorelle. Antiquarian Adolfo de Velasco, the proprietor of a number of art galleries scattered between Andalusia and Morocco, adapted to the peculiar situation by taking lodgings in the old mushroom bed built in the kitchen garden cultivated by the painter. Two gloomy rooms dripping with moisture and still pervaded with the mouldy odour released by growing champignon. What an idea to go live in a place of that ilk with the medina available with all its Oriental charms! But de Velasco is a man who loves to amaze his friends by taking on impossible challenges for that very purpose, thus adding spice to his life with a touch of folly, said to be the mark of a genial personality. The dismay at the purchase of that property was followed by the certainty that de Velasco's surprises were far from over. In a matter of weeks the mushroom bed had been transformed into a spectacular home, conceived as a loft where nature and culture are joined in unexpectedly seamless fashion. The open space is characterised by an orientalist flavour and theatrical atmosphere; thanks to de Velasco's refined taste, the odd little place has ended up resembling a perfectly fine home. The dwelling evokes the delights of the Trianon at Versailles and recalls the curious Chinese Palatset of the castle of Drottingholm in Sweden, where "the gigantic and exceptional nature of the antique objects displayed keep the poverty of the original architecture in the background." The decorative gigantism is hardly a sign of ostentation, instead expressing de Velasco's love for the theatre. "I furnished the house with a scene-designer's touch, leaving nothing to chance." The colour scheme and fabrics, and the placement of statues and paintings are the result of careful thought; in addition, de Velasco made a great number of sketches of the type habitually used by practitioners of the figurative arts prior to taking brush in hand. The more critical voices say the decor falls into the "still life" genre, lacking warmth and intimacy. The fate of the old mushroom bed might have been to become one of many houses "without a soul," dominated by the aestheticism of its owner, as exemplified by the porcelain vases of Asian manufacture placed in niches, the Indian furniture of carved wood reflected in the Venetian mirrors, and the profusion of gilded bronzes. Fortunately, nature intervenes with a beneficial touch. An ancient pepper tree towering in a drawing-room seems almost like a load-bearing pillar, papyruses screen the windows, wisteria hangs down from the balustrades, a vine climbs the walls, and iris, roses and other flowers lend a graceful touch. Years have passed since Majorelle left, but the fruit of his passion for botany lingers on to keep de Velasco company and watch over the wellbeing of the mushroom bed.

In painter Majorelle's old mushroom bed, antique dealer Adolfo de Velasco has given free reign to his two consuming interests, botanical and oriental art, evident in this extraordinary collection of vases from the time of the great Chinese dynasties and East India Company.

This fine cedar door is a vibrant homage to the eighteenth-century cabinet-makers of Syria. Used as an area for relaxation, sitting room and reception hall, the heart of Adolfo de Velasco's palace is the greenhouse. In the middle of the greenhouse, the trunk of an ancient pepper tree acts as an enormous totem keeping watch over the building.

DAR AHLAM

Hidden in the heart of the Palmeraie, Dar Ahlam is one of those rare dwellings that enjoy the privilege of tranquillity and – as a symbol of their status – have chosen discretion and quiet over clamorous worldly celebrations. Dar Ahlam's resident interpreter of this philosophy, now rare in Marrakech, is Tamy Tazy, known as one of the most original and valued creators of fashion at the royal court of Rabat, and among other things, is considered the only person capable of raising caftans and other of Morocco's traditional garments to the rank of art.

The building is seductively simple, comparable to a tasteful winter greenhouse, with a layout suitable for a dollhouse; far from the sumptuous architectural conceptions common in Marrakech today, it represents a special point of reference in the panorama of local twentieth-century architecture. Fifteen years ago nearly everyone firmly rejected the use of pisé walls of clay and straw, as part of a heritage dating from pre-Saharan times discredited by long experience in a fragile medina held captive to the laws of nature. French decorator Jacqueline Foussac was a notable exception, being firmly dedicated to a revival of the ancient technique, convinced as she was that it would prove to be her most reliable ally within the confines of the "Red City." She designed Dar Ahlam with the help of architect Bill Willis. It was planned to be both her home and museum, a synthesis of the clay architecture of Marrakech, which, as the Berbers say, uses the sun for cement. The result was a masterpiece that sublimated the virtues of pisé. Initially, Marrakech was horrified, then merely taken aback: this pisé had a far different appearance than the pitiful look to be found in the narrow streets of the medina. Since then others have followed suit, but today the original Dar Ahlam that revived past splendour is owned by Tamy Tazy, who purchased it with the certainty that Jacqueline Fouassac's small home would be just the place for expressing his passionate interest in the decorative arts of Morocco. His creative vein suggested coating the layer of *tadelakt* with novel creams and browns, including burnt sienna, bold tints that shocked at first only to later become fashionable. His collections of antique fabrics and embroideries remind Tamy Tazy's lucky friends, who are the only ones allowed in the house, of the depth of his attachment to fashion. His innate sense of style has enabled him to work wonders in the Andalusian garden, conceived to pivot around water with its incomparable gift of spreading freshness and music all around as it flows from one basin to the next. The enchanted oasis is as the Koran prescribes, being verdant and bright so as to cheer the spirit at the end of a trying day. This garden, expressing a special adoration for antique roses, contains a profusion of flowers from all over the world. The venation on the back of the petals suggests the handwriting used by Hadjdj An-Numayri in composing his verse. The passionate admirer of the Andalusian garden counselled: "Contemplate with your eyes my elegance and beauty, the marvellous art with which I was built."

It was the desire of the most appreciated of Moroccan stylists to the royal court, Tamy Tazi, to make this winter garden hidden in the *palmaraie* a homage to the country's decorative arts. The ceilings of Tataoui reflect the creativity of the Berber builders, while the carpets of Glaoui and Tazenakt confirm the skill of producers in the Atlas range, where it is customary to pass the long winter evenings weaving wool and silk. The long tradition includes the lace used for bedcovers and the superb old fabrics recovered in Meknes and Fèz, where from time immemorial Morocco's most talented practitioners of the art have been found.

KSAR TALAMANZOU

It was English singer Sting's idea for his fiftieth birthday celebration that brought fame to a Berber village perched on a mountainside of the Atlas range. Prior to the event, only the palm-grove and medina of Marrakech received such consideration, while the thought of actually settling at the foot of Mount Tukbal, where all is bare and plain, never occurred to outsiders. After the birthday party, though, there were those who began to find the *riad* suffocating, with their pretentious palaces rising amidst the palms on the desert's edge. Sting was right: the time had come to get back to authenticity and renew the old adage that states: "To live in happiness, live apart." Thus began the migration in the direction of the Ourika and Asni valleys, which took the more enterprising along the ancient road to Agadir, where only the pomegranates and figs of Barbaria oppose the advance of the sands of the Sahara. Here, at nightfall, the stars join with the distant lights of Marrakech to form a stunning Milky Way. The unsullied landscape illuminates the look of the Berber countrymen. It is impossible to remain indifferent in the face of all this, certainly for someone who normally lives in Paris, as did art expert Jean Yves Barczyk. In no time he was bidding goodbye to his colleagues at the Drouot auction house and closing his gallery specialising in post-Expressionist painting – and off he went on his quest for a personal Eden. The village of Talamanzou beckoned, a *bled* whose authenticity would be the envy of Sting, where the ancient rite of painting cabalistic signs on the sides of the clay houses to ward off evil is still observed. It is a village dominated by a hill where, so it seemed, in the past century the fortress of an influential figure in Berber history had been located. With the snowy Atlas range on one side and the Haouz plain on the other, Jean Yves Barczyk had no qualms: he would make the hill of Talamanzou his Eden, all the more so because of the ruins under the vegetation grown wild. The building stones scattered around obviously indicated bygone wealth, that of the fortress of the *caid* M'Tughi, powerful head of the Berber tribes of the Atlas range. Thanks to the ability of Jean Louis Barczyk, the past began a rebirth. The game of patience provided insights into the skills and wisdom of earlier architects, with the layout of the old buildings having clearly been designed to conserve heat in the wintertime, while the mix of clay and straw used as building materials ensured coolness in the summertime. Windows and doors were arranged out of kilter to increase ventilation. Two years of archaeological research and repairs were required before the former dwelling of the *caid* could be said to have been restored to its former glory, further enhanced by the expert owner's use of the objects he held most dear to adorn it. "The fine old things of life" included carpets found in local bazaars and Berber earthenware purchased from an antique dealer in Marrakech – nothing pretentious, just splashes of colour to highlight the authenticity and simplicity of the quarters. A surprise and a delight. In the entrance to this Eden a golden book invites friends passing through to leave Jean Yves a reminder of the emotions they experienced there. One anonymous pen mused: "And if this dwelling at the end of the world were the anteroom to paradise …"

At the foot of the Atlas Mountains, home of Berber tribes, everyday life is accompanied by age-old rites steeped in sorcery. Ksar Talamanzu was once the refuge of a powerful *caïd* who ruled over the region's mountain tribes.

Reconstructed on the ruins of the ancient dwelling of the *caïd*, the fortress of Talamanzu is exclusively furnished with rustic antiques typical of the Berbers. The bookshelves lining the walls of the entrance are perhaps the loveliest of these items. The same walls have numerous niches that hold terracotta pieces dating from the early twentieth century.

DAR ALHIND

According to ancient legend, "the ardent children of the African earth and sun," meaning the date palms of the Palmeraie of Marrakech, were born a thousand years ago. At that time the sultan Yussef Ben Tachefine, who was looking for a territory to found the capital of the Almoravidi dynasty, encamped on the sandy plain of Haouz. The legend goes on to say that at nightfall Tachefine's warriors whiled away the time munching dates, letting the pits drop where they might. The ones that fell into the holes where their lances had been planted eventually germinated. Centuries later, as if to confirm that the soldiers' banquet of legend had really taken place, the same plain had become a lush oasis with fifty thousand palms. Here American architect and designer Stuart Church and his friend Jaouad Kadiri decided to make a dream come true and express their fascination with Oriental culture and Buddhist philosophy. Thus it was that Dar Alhind came into being, a house pervaded with the spirit and traditions of India, hidden in one of the most picturesque corners of Morocco. Attracted to Tangiers by Paul Bowles, William Burroughs and other members of the Beat Generation, Stuart Church wasted no time in making himself known as an artist in the French colonial villas and the home of American millionaire Malcolm Forbes. While universally admired, no one was swept away by his love for India. "Too bold a venture for a country bent on protecting its native culture." Church's hope of building a palace fit for a maharaja remained a chimera until the day he chanced to meet Jaouad Kadiri, the nonconformist son of a well-to-do Casablanca family. A courageous individual endowed with a healthy dose of cheek, he accepted Church's challenge, aided by the fact that he owned land in the Palmeraie of Marrakech. The Dar Alhind adventure was underway. "The building project was anything but easy," recalls the architect. Kadiri's Islamic roots forced Church to modify the sumptuous elegance of his original scheme and eliminate the windows of the main façade as unacceptable to the Arab world. It then became a copy of a severe *ksur*, one of the fortresses that dot the Dra valley in southern Morocco. But austerity vanishes the moment one sets foot in the *setwan*, the corridor that leads to the *bayt* flooded with natural light from a monumental glass ceiling. The space is in keeping with Oriental tradition, redolent of incense starting at daybreak and lulled all day long by melodies of the zithers. Harmonious volumes and the exuberant colours of the saris, scarves and Gujera fabrics form the basic features of a decor that is always viewed as being functional to water, the key to Stuart Church's work and the leading component of the architectural project. A symbol of purity invaluable for meditation, water has been omnipresent in the Palmeraie of Marrakech ever since the followers of Yussef Ben Tachfine – whom we meet again – had the idea of building a system consisting of a network of *kettara* and *seguia* to bring it all the way from the Atlas Mountains to the city. "A gift of Allah" that Church has made good use of in a succession of fountains and basins that disappear into an olive orchard that forms the natural boundary of Dar Alhind. At night they are seen to best advantage at the time when the generator that supplies power for the property falls silent. Then thousands of candles are reflected in the water of the basins, while the frogs, just as in India at the same moment, begin their concert. And Dar Alhind gives itself up to the desires of Siddharta.

The veranda designed by American architect Stuart Church introduces
guests to the delightful sight of the most beautiful palaces of Rajasthan,
the favourite place of Jauad Kadiri, owner of Dar Alhind.

Theatrical atmosphere in one of the rooms reserved for female guests at Dar Alhind. The light curtains of pink silk, Venetian mirrors and fragrant incense all contribute to make guests feel like Indian princesses … or Moroccan odalisques.

Palais Rhoul

A sanctuary of beauty, peace and serenity, Palazzo Rhoul – whose hallmark is its exquisite nature – is numbered among those private dwellings open to travellers. Long before it became a privileged stopping place for exceptional guests, this fascinating building belonged to a noble family of Oujda eager to escape the rigours of the climate of northern Morocco.

The Rhoul family, one of the country's most prominent, has managed to express its openness towards the world while at the same time showing itself to be an attentive keeper of Maghrebian traditions, creating the conditions for the art of good living without equal in Marrakech, including the enchanted atmosphere of the palace that places it on the outer limits of reality bordering on a fairytale world. Palazzo Rhoul is an "earthly paradise where the spirit reawakens, the soul is appeased and the body finds repose," explains Sacha Rhoul, the host of a dwelling that arose in the heart of Palmeraie approximately a quarter of a century ago, fruit of the fertile imagination of architect Aziz Lamghari. Following his unchained fancy, he reproduced the residence of Pontius Pilate in Galilee, a splendid replica work with Corinthian columns reflected in a romantic basin.

The construction is embellished with the same elements that adorned Pontius Pilate's home. In this architecture, consistent with history, the bedrooms are complete with secret doors that kindle the imagination and conjure up the image of concubines slipping into the master's apartments. Thoughts wander and dreams chase after one another in Palazzo Rhoul, as one passes from the delightful little Zen drawing room, where the oneiric radiates towards infinity, to the library featuring leather and wood, and on to the baths carved from Syrian marble in keeping with old Moorish custom.

The impression is unchanging: at Palazzo Rhoul the clock seems to have stopped, a delightful sensation derived from the decor that includes paintings by great artists, valuable antiquities from East and West, rare books and countless knick-knacks that suggest the centuries of prominence of the Rhoul family.

The suspended time is pervaded by the scent of parchment, the warm presence of the wainscoting, the fragrance of the beeswax; it is stopped by the charm of the water, the element that governs life in the palazzo with its languid sparkling that reaches as far as the salons with its swift perpetual purling that accompanies the life of the hotel. The water disappears as if by magic among the palms, rare essences and rose garden – the fragrant shady spots of Palazzo Rhoul that are complemented by shady spots dedicated to music: the kiosks of Roman inspiration and the pavilions in the garden, where in the evening when the muezzins call out, Rhoul's harps and cellos begin the concert.

In the dream setting of Palazzo Rhoul, conceived by architect Aziz Lamghari, guests indulge in the wholesome delights of the *hammam*, a sumptuous architecture considered the most striking of its kind in Marrakech.

DAR TAYDA

No doubt about it: the Hispano-Moorish architectural canons that have dominated Marrakech for over a millennium – meaning from the beginning of the Almohadi dynasty – are beginning to vacillate under the blows of extravagant anti-conformist Francesco de la Pinta, designer and architect. This is a man who takes pleasure in shunning ideas handed down from the past and upsetting tradition. He is a man who has made outer space the ideal material of his creative energy. His intense feeling for the cosmos has found an outlet in the Moroccan desert, the perfect place to build the avant-garde vessel of Dar Tayda, right in the middle of the palms of Marrakech. The building, heavily influenced by the work of Mexican architect Barragan, is characterised by rigorous lines and outsized proportions that enhance a structure of evident Hispano-Mexican inspiration. Some of its features are to be found in the ranches of Texas and southern California. Dar Tayda has the appearance of a gigantic construction of cubes, some poised skyward, and others sunk in the ground. Huge picture windows and others that are mere slits join the horizontal and vertical components. Far from Oriental splendour, the complex is more akin to a "contemporary monastery." The atmosphere is Zen; the furnishing Minimalist, as is evident in a dining room bare enough to recall the refectory of a Cistercian abbey. This unadorned architecture – uniformly plastered and painted ochre with a hint of pink – lends itself to the decorative approach of Francesco de la Pinta with his predilection for primitive African art and antique furniture from India. Here the furnishings are a clear reference to the life of the Dogon population of Mali and the skill of the cabinet-makers of Rajastan, including funeral masks with cabalistic symbols carved in the jacaranda wood, rustic doors and camel ploughs used for tables, in addition to rugs, the number of which is an accurate indication of the owner's passion for them. It was this passion that led him to track down craftsmen believed no longer in existence, but who are in fact still at work employing archaic rug-making techniques. Those from Mauritania, for instance, still know how to weave reeds and leather to good effect. In the mid-Atlas region, rug makers manage to give their commendable work an ethnic touch while at the same time taking inspiration from the tapestries of Gobelin. In short, Dar Tayda is cloaked in a simplicity that is precious in the best sense of the word, shunning anything that might compromise the essential "poverty" of the place that is unabashedly on display. The apparent emptiness underscores Dar Tayda's reason for being, its "attachment to the cosmic universe," in the words of its author. "Here stone, light and silence mingle in space." The vagabond spirit goes back to Yussef Ben Tachefine, founder of the Palmeraie of Marrakech, for whom magic was an integral part of everyday life. One's thoughts turn to the unidentified objects regularly seen at night in the Sahara. The spirit is capable of daring to think the unthinkable. Dar Tayda confirms that, for all its space-station style, Francesco de la Pinta is much more than the "spaceman of architecture" his friends fondly call him.

The Minimalist ambience and Zen spirit of Dar Tayda are testimony to the arrival of avant-garde architecture
in Marrakech. The sober lines, monumental volumes and austere decor are proof that oriental ostentation
is not the only face of the "Daughter of the Desert."

DAR SOUKI

Infinite space, unspoiled nature, silence, and the deep tranquillity that regenerates and renews the forgotten pleasure of reflection are what prompted French medical luminary Gilles Blanchard to take refuge in the wildest and least known corner of Palmeraie. His Dar Souki, infused with light and open on the horizon, reflects the owner's fascination with different cultures around the world; it is related to an architecture that might have sprung from the mind of Potamone of Alexandria – an eclectic architecture skilfully incorporating different styles that bear witness to construction over time.

Blanchard's long stay in Japan is reflected in a touch of the Zen spirit here in Marrakech, while a visit to Africa is reflected in the tribal elements of the *dar*. At a superficial reading, the unusual, disparate juxtapositions might seem likely to disturb the eye of an aesthete. Yet Dar Souki pleases, pervaded as it is by an indisputable elegance, a product of the omnipresent windows that have a way of bringing the outdoors in so as to integrate the cactus garden and interior to the point that the overall effect resembles the cloister of a Benedictine monastery.

Yes, Dar Souki is unreservedly eclectic. As one gradually adjusts to the spatial element, it at last becomes possible to give an identity to the construction, which resembles an immense aviary of African inspiration enveloped in the atmosphere of a Japanese temple – African in the primitive line described by the bricks of the vault of the large main room like an aviary, and Japanese in the narrow basins framed by pergolas open to the sky.

The structural eclecticism provides the proper setting for highlighting Gilles Blanchard's passion for contemporary design, which stresses tonality over form and materials. Intense colours, such as the powerful reds and blues of Armani's sofas, were chosen by the owner for the specific purpose of calling attention away from the presence of the windows and creating the impression that the two colours are actually vast stretches of poppies and bluebottles planted in the middle of the aviary. The optical effect leads one to conclude that the garden is the true protagonist of the interior decoration of Dar Souki. Whether the garden is in the aviary or the aviary is in the garden matters little. The birds have grasped the spirit of the house: goldfinches and swallows live there in peace, happy to be in a home that is not a cage.

First Edition September 2005